FOUR FOOT TWO

Building a New Business

D.H. OSBORNE

CONTENTS

FOUR FOOT TWO

First Published: March 30, 2026

Published by: OliveStrength Productions LLC

A Note from Me to You

Hi there. I'm so glad you're reading this book.

In order to truly win, you need a team.

And in my experience, the best team member you can add is God!

In business, before making big decisions, sending over a quote, or in the middle of a challenging project-

I consult with my Team.

I pray, lean into God's spirit, and request wisdom, knowledge, strength, favor, ability...

Whatever it is that I am lacking, I go to Jesus and ask for HELP!

As a kid, I learned to love reading and learning in a 4'2" wide walk-in closet that was my bedroom. In that little space, I read hundreds (if not thousands) of books on my bed, a green military/camp style bunking cot.

Foreword

Barbra J. Osborne

Counting the Cost....

Will your vision for a new business be sustainable?

This *will* be a place frequently visited with your mind's eye.

If I may, let me share a glimpse into my world- the wife of a driven and passionate business owner.

One might very well consider this journey to be a lonely one.

Building a business takes time, focus, determination, and sacrifice from not just the owner, but the family as a whole.

Counting the Cost of long hours, that suddenly turn into long years, is not about the season you find yourself in, but about the success you are striving for.

As much courage as it takes to start a business, an Entrepreneur's partner must be willing to stay strong in the valleys of growth.

I personally have never approached my husband with a heart of resentment for taking the time demanded of him to build a legacy.

Being an Entrepreneur... It wasn't a decision made out of personal vanity, but one determined to create a beautiful foundation for our future.

First generation wealth builders have to fight through barriers, and pay prices not paid by past generations, to have a chance to reap where others have never sowed.

Businesses are built with integrity and honor, creating an environment to better our communities.

For that Cost, you must be willing to be a team at home, helping to grow a vision for that brand.

You will learn the importance of being intentional with your quality time with your family while also giving your business everything it will require from you.

I believe that compared to many others, our story is unique, but I'm so thankful for the lessons life has taught my husband and I during his 20 years of building our legacy.

While reading this book, please understanc reward of Counting the Cost.

Understand that systems, when in place, al Success.

Understand that, in every hardship and grov there is a hope for a steady business.

As you study the systems shared throughout the be confident that your success is worth Cou Cost.

Be Strong. Be Willing. Be Diligent. Be Brave.

This book can help you break free from your present life circumstances, and turn ideas and dreams into actions, plans, and a new reality.

I started with next to nothing, but after 20+ years have made some headway in this world, giving my children a stable home base to grow from.

Some people think being poor is just about not having enough money...

But it's more than that.

*Just like being successful, being poor starts with how **you** think and feel.*

Your attitude is one of the only things you *can* control. It's why some people can sell shoes to a population that is barefoot, and others are convinced there's no demand for their product–

Attitude and vision define your actions.

After you read this book, it will be *your* turn to use these tools to make your own life better and to help others along the way.

Some of these concepts are mentioned more than once in this book.

So, make a choice today.

Choose to do the work.

The work on your business, on your skills, on your friendships, and on Yourself.

Choose to be Excellent-

Your community is counting on you.

I really, *really* want you to succeed.

I know what it feels like to have a mental breakdown, to feel hopeless, and to have almost no friends and no money. I've had less than $40 to buy diapers and food for my family for a whole week. I've also been able to spend way more than that on a nice vacation.

I want you to have success.

Success for me is acting on my Faith. It's living in and following the will of God, living a submitted, modest life with the authority and power to equip and help others.

If you decide that owning a business isn't for you after reading this book, that's okay!

But ***please*** don't hold anyone else back!

Give them this book. Share their business posts on Facebook. Buy from them. Help them get started. Support them quietly, and publicly-

Foreword

Barbra J. Osborne

Counting the Cost....

Will your vision for a new business be sustainable?

This *will* be a place frequently visited with your mind's eye.

If I may, let me share a glimpse into my world- the wife of a driven and passionate business owner.

One might very well consider this journey to be a lonely one.

Building a business takes time, focus, determination, and sacrifice from not just the owner, but the family as a whole.

Counting the Cost of long hours, that suddenly turn into long years, is not about the season you find yourself in, but about the success you are striving for.

2 | FOUR FOOT TWO

As much courage as it takes to start a business, an Entrepreneur's partner must be willing to stay strong in the valleys of growth.

I personally have never approached my husband with a heart of resentment for taking the time demanded of him to build a legacy.

Being an Entrepreneur... It wasn't a decision made out of personal vanity, but one determined to create a beautiful foundation for our future.

First generation wealth builders have to fight through barriers, and pay prices not paid by past generations, to have a chance to reap where others have never sowed.

Businesses are built with integrity and honor, creating an environment to better our communities.

For that Cost, you must be willing to be a team at home, helping to grow a vision for that brand.

You will learn the importance of being intentional with your quality time with your family while also giving your business everything it will require from you.

I believe that compared to many others, our story is unique, but I'm so thankful for the lessons life has taught my husband and I during his 20 years of building our legacy.

While reading this book, please understand the great reward of Counting the Cost.

Understand that systems, when in place, always bring Success.

Understand that, in every hardship and growing pain, there is a hope for a steady business.

As you study the systems shared throughout these pages, be confident that your success is worth Counting the Cost.

Be Strong. Be Willing. Be Diligent. Be Brave.

A Note from Me to You

Hi there. I'm so glad you're reading this book.

In order to truly win, you need a team.

And in my experience, the best team member you can add is God!

In business, before making big decisions, sending over a quote, or in the middle of a challenging project-

I consult with my Team.

I pray, lean into God's spirit, and request wisdom, knowledge, strength, favor, ability...

Whatever it is that I am lacking, I go to Jesus and ask for HELP!

As a kid, I learned to love reading and learning in a 4'2" wide walk-in closet that was my bedroom. In that little space, I read hundreds (if not thousands) of books on my bed, a green military/camp style bunking cot.

This book can help you break free from your present life circumstances, and turn ideas and dreams into actions, plans, and a new reality.

I started with next to nothing, but after 20+ years have made some headway in this world, giving my children a stable home base to grow from.

Some people think being poor is just about not having enough money...

But it's more than that.

Just like being successful, being poor starts with how ***you*** *think and feel.*

Your attitude is one of the only things you *can* control. It's why some people can sell shoes to a population that is barefoot, and others are convinced there's no demand for their product–

Attitude and vision define your actions.

After you read this book, it will be *your* turn to use these tools to make your own life better and to help others along the way.

Some of these concepts are mentioned more than once in this book.

So, make a choice today.

Choose to do the work.

The work on your business, on your skills, on your friendships, and on Yourself.

Choose to be Excellent-

Your community is counting on you.

I really, *really* want you to succeed.

I know what it feels like to have a mental breakdown, to feel hopeless, and to have almost no friends and no money. I've had less than $40 to buy diapers and food for my family for a whole week. I've also been able to spend way more than that on a nice vacation.

I want you to have success.

Success for me is acting on my Faith. It's living in and following the will of God, living a submitted, modest life with the authority and power to equip and help others.

If you decide that owning a business isn't for you after reading this book, that's okay!

But ***please*** don't hold anyone else back!

Give them this book. Share their business posts on Facebook. Buy from them. Help them get started. Support them quietly, and publicly-

And no matter what, always tell the truth and keep your promises.

Over the past 20 years, I've worked my way out of poverty. Now, I want to share the tools and ideas that can help you succeed.

Mark this book up!

Write down your dreams, your hopes, your fears, your angry moments, your frustrations...

This is supposed to be as much of a manual for success as it is meant to be a gift to help fellow entrepreneurs.

Let's Grow!

CHAPTER 1

The Secret to Success Is Hard Work

People tell me that being a business owner isn't for everyone. Maybe that's true, but it's been the driving force of my life for the last 25+ years, so it's hard for me to try to connect with anything that doesn't include a mindset of growth, promise, and ownership.

Being a successful business owner **is** a choice. On social media, some people make it look "easy." They post pictures of their boats, nice dinners, and fancy trips. That's the "After."

What about the "Before?!"

From what I've seen, people who succeed in business know how to work hard.

This hard work is what I call "*The Grind.*"

It means you keep going when things are slow and boring. You push through the bad times. And when things are good, you make careful and smart choices, over and over again. It means you take the right chances and see them through to the end.

The Grind is real. The good things that come from it are real, too. But the risks and the potential losses are not to be ignored.

Story Time

On one occasion, in my early 30's, this really hit home. My wife Barbra and I are active in our local church, and there is a yearly conference that we attend and support. On top of our regularly scheduled responsibilities, this is a wonderful and yet very full time of the year for us.

I had taken on a larger contract for my company a few months before the conference, and unfortunately, things did not go as planned. Working on a hard day count to wrap up the job, we were about 17 days over what I had anticipated was to be our finish date. My helper and I put in some LONG hours on that job; we stayed until 10:30PM one night, just to hit a benchmark towards completion.

FINALLY towards the end of the project one afternoon, I started shaking.

Now in Florida, this is not a super uncommon occurrence- Whether "The Bear" gets you (heat exhaustion) or your blood sugars simply crash, an "old man lunch" will usually pick me up; a pack of peanut-butter crackers, and a cold can of Coke.

I took a little break and had a snack, but I still couldn't stop shaking. I went inside, put my toolbelt back on, and tried to set the screw.

No joy.

I couldn't install a single screw in the drywall properly; it just kept turning sideways.

At this point, as the kids would say, I was "cooked."

Here I was, over a decade of trade experience, business owner, trying to make things happen–

I had literally worked until I couldn't.

So, we packed it in, and I let Barbra (my wife) know that we were going to go away for a few days.

We got a nice little hotel room, where the kids could fish and enjoy the outdoors.

Side Quest

Their fishing bait bucket was left out overnight- IN THE BACK OF MY TRUCK. It filled the entire area with the putrid smell of rotting shrimp. That was nice touch. ;)

While my family enjoyed the pool, the beach, and fishing, I laid in bed and did nothing. I simply had to lay there and rest the majority of the time. It wasn't fair to my family, and it wasn't fair to myself.

By NOT being disciplined and taking time off, my body decided that time off was what it **was** going to get.

Period.

Moral of the story? Those of us that are "sick," that LIKE to work, have to be disciplined in our down time the way many folks must be disciplined in doing their work.

Action-

Do you need to focus on working hard on being intentional with your work ethic, or on your scheduled down time?

Do you plan ahead for your health and family needs as a business owner?

CHAPTER 2

A Hard Truth: Nobody Cares

(And More Money Doesn't Make All Your Problems Go Away!)

Ugly Fact- Nobody Cares.

* *Adapted Material From Greatest Things I Learned as an Entrepreneur* *

This chapter might not feel very nice at first.

I know, you've got your new business cards, handed out flyers, and you've asked all your friends to "Like" your social media pages...

And now I'm going to tell you something that might be hard to hear:

Nobody Cares.

Yup.

It is True.

You see, in business, the most important thing is an "Equitable Value Exchange."

That's a fancy way of saying that when you give someone something they need, they give you something of appropriate value in return.

In business, that can be a good, service, or actionable knowledge. (Think lawyer, business coach, consultant, etc.)

Businesses fail when this trade isn't fair or clear.

As the business owner, failure typically happens when you didn't give the other party what you promised at the time and *in the way* you agreed to do so.

Or, they just didn't understand what they were getting.

When your phone rings, it's because a customer wants something from you. That said, I have had to confront this mindset before–

"They don't really care how nice you sound on the phone or how friendly you are. They just want what you're selling."

Actually, they **DO** care!

You can disqualify yourself from providing the needed goods or services by being rude, indifferent, or coming across as a novice.

What folks really want is what you are going to do for *them*, and how you make them feel in the process. In my service business, they typically want to know two things: when can I fix their drywall, and how much will it cost? That's usually what matters, especially at the start.

This idea that "Nobody Cares" is true in many parts of your business.

- **Your supplier messed up?** Your customer doesn't care. They made a deal with YOU for a certain product/service at a certain time. If you don't deliver, you have broken the deal.

- **Something sad happened in your family?** Your customer will feel bad for you, but they still have a hole in their ceiling that they want fixed. Or a wedding cake to be delivered. Or a business valuation report to produce. The client still expects you to do the job you promised to do. Your problems are just getting in the way of what they need, and what you agreed to do.

Storytime-

COVID was quite the experience.

After getting the "real bad one" (where I had a fever, lost my sense of smell, and was laid up for weeks) I finally recovered, and went to work. Finishing the repair job, I headed to a late "little bite" at my favorite local lunch spot. Judging the distance of a vehicle in the left-hand lane behind me, I made my way into the turn lane, and proceeded through an intersection.

Well, most of the way through-

My world *exploded*.

The crew cab truck was struck by not one, not two, but three vehicles that hit my vehicle and trailer.

The impact was so forceful, the 2" drop-hitch receiver for towing was sheared in half. One safety chain snapped, another ripped free of the trailer weld. However, the trailer was still towable. So, I picked up the tools off the asphalt that had managed to be so freely ejected from the access door in the nose of the trailer, grabbed a piece of 1/8" luan, and slapped it into the gaping hole where there *used* to be a door. My church dad Eddie Sheffield came and towed it to his place.

I got a rental truck, and less than 24 hours later I was on a new jobsite, keeping our word to a roofing company that had us fulfilling their warranty repair needs.

All the airbags went off on the passenger / impact side, and by the Mercy of God, I escaped with nothing but a small strawberry bruise on my left shoulder. (My head was good and scrambled for a few days though.) Thankfully, there were no fatalities, and everyone walked away.

Because WHY?

Because I gave my Word.

At the end of the day, your problems are YOUR problems. Do whatever you can to keep your word.

Does that make sense? This is a foundational rule in business.

Nobody Cares.

Ugly Fact-

More Money DOES NOT mean money problems go away.

As you go through this book and your business, and make your money, you'll have more solutions to find.

Your standard of living will either cripple you, or empower you as a new business owner.

Forget "Keeping up with the Neighbors."

It's our OWN appetites that must be curbed.

I'm guilty.

(You might have some cookie crumbs on your hands as well.)

We all have emotional triggers; situations that we aren't good at walking through logically. Temperance, with a focus on your WIIFM and WHY will keep you from many bad decisions.

Your foundational identified goals and needs can **also** serve as "reasons" for financial instruments and frankly, just bad debt.

A modest, calculated, even sacrificial mindset does a better job of serving an entrepreneur than one of simply reacting out of frustration or fear.

Decide what is "Good Enough" NOW.

Not after you've doubled or tripled your sales, and have a couple more dollars to be responsible for.

Your (and your family's!) standard of living will directly impact the financial resources and decisions of your business.

CHAPTER 3

Two Big Questions You Must Answer

Now that you understand that it's your job to solve problems and keep your promises, let's figure out if you should even own a business.

Before you start, you need to answer two big questions.

WIIFM?

What's **I**n **I**t **F**or **M**e?

Why?

Why do you want to do this?

Ugly Fact-

If you can't answer these questions clearly, first to yourself and then to others face-to-face, you are not ready to own a business.

Without strong answers, you won't have the power to keep going when things get hard. You won't have a good reason to keep your promises- the ones you make to yourself, and the ones you make to everyone else.

So, what IS in it for you?

You get responsibility. You get heartache, headaches, and an unrealistic sense of urgency to care so deeply and passionately for something that literally no one else *can*-

It is ***YOUR*** creation.

Like a four-year-old's painted rock, or a sculptor's masterpiece of many years, your business is your creation and you are "all in." The highs are higher, and the depths are OHHH so much deeper than what we experience when we are a corporate team member or employee!

Much like a clutch in a car, everything can be working fine, and then a little pressure and heat gets applied, and you think "It's ok, I've got this." Things can still chug along, for a while. However, you grind those gears too much, you push the limits hard and fast and long enough, something IS gonna give.

And in my experience, when it does go bad, it is catastrophic.

What DOES being a business owner get you?

Being a business owner gives you freedom... of choice.

You get to make choices. If a customer is rude, you can choose not to work with them. You can politely say, "I don't think we are a good fit for your project." You can choose to give that elderly couple a discount on their repair. You can choose to be gracious, and return a deposit that you are contractually entitled to.

Your **WHY** is the core reason you are doing this.

Maybe your answer to "Why" is because "you want to make money." *Why?* To pay your bills. *Why?* So you can live in a safe place. *Why?* Because you remember what it was like to be poor, and you want a better life for your kids.

Money alone won't keep you going.

But a strong WHY will!

It's like a deep track in the road that keeps your wagon wheels straight, even when the wind is blowing hard, and the rain obscures the landmarks. Now imagine the horses break away from the wagon, or die, or get stolen, and you're left with nothing but a load that you can hardly move on your own, and not much in the way of help available to get it to its destination.

Your undeniable WHY keeps you soldiering on with purpose.

Without a Why, you don't have a business–

You have a hobby that will eventually fade away.

Action–

Identify and Write Down YOUR WIIFM and WHY.

Now, read them out loud.

What do you wish you could change?

What SHOULD you change?

CHAPTER 4

The Building Blocks of a Business

Disclaimer

Much like a dealer is released from the responsibility of what happens with a vehicle after it is purchased, the following tools and decisions in this chapter can do a WORLD of good, or lead to a life crisis of epic proportions.

You Have Been Warned

You might be thinking that this is the same type of advice given in every business book. *Be on time. Keep your word. Don't steal.*

You're right!

Ugly Fact-

If you don't do these basic things, your business will fail. It would be like trying to drive a car without ever putting gas in it. So, here are the basic building blocks you need:

- **Pick One Thing and Be Great at It:** Are you going to make soap, fix air conditioners, or sell lemonade? Choose one thing to focus on. Get really, really good at that one thing. You can always add more later. Do ONE thing with excellence, and then you can add to your goods or services from there.

- **Be Specific**- "Full Service, We Do it All, Anything to do with..." isn't telling people what you do or offer- It's an invitation for people to tune out.

- **Set Up Your Business Correctly:** You will need to open a business bank account to keep your business money separate from your personal money. Beyond a flashy name, graphics, advertising, you've got to keep the "backbone" straight. Non-negotiable here. To keep yourself out of legal, business, and accounting trouble, set up a separate business bank account that ALL deposits go to. This ensures accurate tracking. No one ends up wondering "Did we get paid, or not?" Many banks now offer remote check deposits- this is very convenient when you're a smaller outfit, and you can't stand "one more errand." (We go over this in more depth in Chapter 15.)

- **Plan Your Operations:** When will you be open? Will you travel to customers, or will they come to you? What are your prices? How will people pay you? *It is very important to have a written agreement, or contract, for your work.*

- **Be Great with Customers:** Always answer the phone! And if you miss a call, call them right back. Let people know when you are on your way. It shows you care.

- **Be Professional:** Be respectful in a customer's home or business. Always clean up after yourself. In my line of work, a clean job site shows that you are a true professional. Always leave a place cleaner than you found it.

- **Focus on Your Market-** Are you selling to businesses? To homeowners/traditional in-person traffic? Are you serving people online?

In my area, general contractors will typically find the person to do the job for the least amount of money. That's cost leadership; not our core value exchange/offering approach. So, DTC (Direct to Consumer) is our approach, as a rule. Even when we work in commercial or industrial settings, it's a very specific need that we facilitate.

For us, we look to serve folks with a drywall repair or replacement need with a HIGH opportunity cost. That means they really, *really* care about how the repair looks, and/or the professional standards of cleanliness, service, and licensure provided. As such, we refer out and/or screen the needs of a lot of potential clients.

With apologies to the vegetarians joining here, we offer filet; not hamburger.

There is NOTHING wrong with offering a hamburger/commodity level of service or goods.

Just be consistent!

Chain restaurants of the fast food variety are wildly successful not because they have great food, but because they consistently deliver an identified need at an approachable price point.

Storytime-

Rufus was a big hairy mutt.

Legitimately, more horse than hound.

Irish wolfhound, to be precise, as I recall. I seem to remember him being pretty kind, and lovable.

It's hard to say really, because during the course of carrying materials, tools, etc. in the home for repairs, I received a call.

It was Rufus.

More specifically, Rufus' parents.

Evidently, without us knowing-

RUFUS GOT OUT OF THE HOUSE AND WAS HAVING A BIG OL' TIME IN THE NEIGHBORHOOD.

So, the kind neighbors got him to their place, and called the homeowner we were working for-

Who then called me.

Now, I'm pretty sure this little escapade was NOT this "Good Boy's" first time in the Great Big Outdoors without a leash, but finding out a pet is missing from the owner that ISN'T at home before YOU know the pet is missing?

Is.

Well...

Not Good.

Pay attention to details, and make sure all pets, small children, and family members are accounted for.

Rufus...

What tools, transportation/ resources are you going to use/need?

This subject alone really deserves an entire book!

Whether you are making ice-cream, welding steel girders, or building websites, there are core things you must have to DO the work...

And when things break, wear out, run out, you've got to have a plan, or you're not going to be able to deliver your product/service.

And that means you're not going to get paid.

Don't focus on buying EVERYTHING new, or even all at once, but focus on being able to consistently deliver what you promised.

How will you do your work? What tools and transportation will you need? Start with what you need to do a quality job/deliver a good product, and be willing to grow with the business.

What's your supply line? Where are you getting the things that you need?

This goes along with the prior point made and where relationships and communication can really pay off. Typically, one can secure 10%, 20% discounts (or more!)

for volume, or simply because you're operating a commercial account versus a traditional consumer. Don't single source EVERYTHING, but where you can develop loyalty and relationships with local businesses, it pays off in both access and the bottom line in the long run.

Storytime-

I've had new and used vehicles/tools over the years, depending on what season I was in, and what the local market would provide. Simply having a commercial account at an auto parts store can save you over 20% on many items. (Frank, we love you. Thank you for always being kind to us!) A standard deduction for shop supplies/ plastic and tape nets north of 15% off of the full retail price. Keep on top of your pricing, keep the corporate office on point and honest, communicate with your local sales representative, and you'll be in a great position to make money!

- **Know Your Collaborators and Fellow Market Servicers-** Who else is in that industry? How are they pricing their product/services? Do they have traditional slow times? Is there an ability to serve them/refer them to projects/clients that aren't a good fit for you?

So much to unpack here. *Collaboration happens at the top, competition at the bottom.* Nobody wants to give away their bread and butter business. It affects how they are able to provide for their own needs. But solving challenges for clients and fellow contractors alike (with a humble attitude) goes a long way in establishing mutually beneficial relationships.

Storytime-

I have a GREAT relationship with many local drywall contractors throughout our coverage area. Why? Communication! My company operates in a specific niche of a single trade- drywall repair and replacement. As such, we NEED to be able to refer folks in the community to other professionals that can properly serve their needs. When I needed somewhere to drop off a vehicle for 9 days because the car rental company didn't have a secured guest lot, I called up my buddy Danny at the supply yard, and he made it happen. That's the power of relationship- *it makes things happen.*

Our drywall company is known as "The Brain Surgeon of Drywall Repair." Well, guess what? "Surgeons" don't know it all, we're constantly learning!

Travis Boucher is our local "Professor." He is the living "Text Book" we go to when we have a hunch, or random question, but don't really know the answer. You know how empowering it is to know that another pro will pick up the phone and help you, in good faith, and not try to sabotage you? We have benefitted so much from this relationship! So, as a rule, we make it a point to share our knowledge with others as well.

- **What are the legal requirements? Do you need a license**? Do you have a partnership? What insurance do you need to carry? What are the permitting requirements for your good/service?

Do your research on this. Every municipality can be different. In Florida, I've been in business long enough to be exposed to several changes of professional oversight and operating requirements. (AKA the laws changed!) Communicate with town, county, state, and even federal guidelines as appropriate to ensure you are operating within the legal obligations of your business.

- **Business Credit Card and Credit Lines-** Can you handle it? Do you know how to effectively use credit? If you can, don't pay cash, unless it's a 2-1, 3-1 ratio. Meaning if the purchase would usually cost $100, you get it for $50, or $33. This flies in the face of many cash-centric business models, but there is a caveat- run your credit like it IS cash! This accurately allows you to take advantage of a true 1-2% average cash back, helps greatly with tracking expenses, and insulates your business from fraud. A $6,000 errant charge on a credit card? That's pretty easily handled. $6,000 missing from the business checking account? That's not good.

- **What are your days and hours of operation?** Are you mobile, or a brick and mortar location?

This MATTERS.

Stick to your guns, and be consistent. If you offer a 24/7 service, do it with consistency. If you only are open 3 nights a week from 4-7 PM as a pop-up tent, **BE THERE.** Folks will put up with a lot of things, but inconsistency is NOT one of them.

Storytime-

Tommy Lea (a local service business owner) and I have been doing business back and forth for YEARS. One time, he passed a GREAT referral along to me, and I stepped out of an obligation to take the phone call...

And then promptly forgot all about it.

I was at church. This taught me an important lesson. Keep the main thing, the main thing. Most of the time, 99.9% of the time, a phone call, text, email can wait. Divided concentration is a recipe for disaster.

Long story short, I GHOSTED the referral. They talked to Tommy about the no call/ no show, and he called and asked me "What happened?"

Our system is set up in triplicate- We text the client the appointment, email the client the appointment, AND put it on our Google calendar. Because I had stepped out of the engagement and headed right back in, I neglected to do ANY of the scheduling!

We "ate the frog," completely took full responsibility for the situation, called the client back, apologized profusely, and then were selected to provide our services. We gave a very nice "THANK YOU" gift to Tommy in return for not just referring us, but sticking by us when there was an "oopsie."

GET A PAYROLL SERVICE.

Do you have employees? Are you handling payroll in house, or are you having a firm take care of it?

This is such a great way to build value, insulate your company, and stay focused on what truly matters. Chad Filley is our GUY in Florida! He makes it so simple to onboard new team members, and keeps all the paperwork correct at the state and federal level. There are some absolute horror stories with this-

Do your homework, have a backup plan in place to be able to pay folks if something goes wrong, and run your business in a legal fashion.

- **Establish forms of payment.** Do you accept Credit Cards as a form of payment? What are your payment terms to clients? What about vendors, subcontractors, and suppliers?

In today's world, your business needs to be able to accept credit cards, and do so securely. Whether integrated into your billing app, QuickBooks, or a stand-alone mobile or hardline terminal, card payment is a major part of folks entering into business with contractors and those that sell goods.

Don't ONLY look for a low rate, but consider- What does the dispute process entail if/when someone decides to go to their credit card company and reverse the charge? And, double check your compliance as well, with ADA Act parameters.

- **Have a Written Contract.** Do you have a contract for goods/ services rendered? Is it hardcopy, a PDF, or both?

(The answer is "yes, by the end of this book, I will have a contract in place for my clients.")

A contract is the warmest, most genuine handshake that you can offer someone else.

A good contract defines the exchange of value that is being entered into, and lets all parties know what the scope/ amount of the product or good is, what the expectations of delivery and timeline are, and what the consequences will be if this agreement is not kept. (Breached, in fancy language.)

- **Brand**- Establish a recognizable, easily identifiable brand. This is almost as important as your WIIFM and WHY. Once you get this locked down, you can begin to represent the values and service of your company with a singular image.

Case in Point: Coca-Cola versus Enron. Two famous names, two WILDLY different emotional reactions to them. And once you dig into the history of them, those views have RADICALLY changed back and forth over the years! Your colors, logo, and language need to be *consistent.*

- **Logo Generation Creation**- Fiverr, 99designs.com or comparable are great! Start by looking at your industry, to see what is catchy/appealing. Then, what makes you tick/what is it that makes you stand out? What tells people that you're here to stay, to serve them, to make a difference?

Less is MORE-

A simple, eye-catching logo with a few visual elements is effective; super busy graphics, obscure text, etc. is not beneficial! It might be appealing to you, make you feel good, but it won't gain *good* visibility.

Storytime-

With my first business at 12, my mom helped me make up some little fliers with Popeye-esque arms adding visual appeal. "Muscles for Money" netted me about $600 that summer, raking lava rock and pulling weeds in the hot New Mexico sun. Fast forward some years later on, Danny's Detail was an auto detailing enterprise I had for about a year. Again, I had no real lasting logo integration, and closed up shop. With DRR Drywall Repair, I had different evolving logos, until I spent about $375 and paid a local marketing company to give me a design / logo facelift.

Best money outside of my marriage license I ever spent.

When we started up a sister company some years later, one of the first things we did was utilize local talent and 99designs.com to get a positive outcome. In about a week, we went from concept to delivered logo. A great logo is like a banner, a "rally point," if you will. Your product and service offerings rally around it. Make it good, simple, and clean. Don't be afraid to tweak it, but be consistent.

- **Business Cards & Vinyl Decals** - A local print shop is YOUR guy for business cards! (Eric Burrus) Ideally, you'll find someone with some design ability. Vinyl graphics for storefront and vehicle windows, and lettering on vehicles works well.

Wrap or Vinyl- Full wraps are the "in" thing now- look around, and you'll see any number of vehicles with business info on the side. The sweet spot for ROI that we stand behind is a *partial* wrap and/ or vinyl lettering that is tastefully done. This usually is about 1/3 the cost of a full wrap. It looks nice, and still gives you an advertising element and air of professional competence.

A clean, legible business card is what you need! Your phone number, website, and a clear explanation of what you do should be on it.

Ugly Fact-

If it isn't producing positive market response with accompanying sales, it's a want, not a need. If you get guilted into a full wrap on a vehicle just because "all the cool kids are doing it," you just got duped. Be incredibly calculated when you make the decisions for financial outlay with your marketing. Marketing dollars spent are wasted if they are not compelling your audience to purchase your goods or service.

- **Website**- Pay someone to do this. Have it in a WordPress (or like) format/platform. Hosting should be under $500 a year, with changes to the website included. *Make sure you OWN the site outright.* A decent 3-5 page website is going to cost you $1500-$3000 properly built. Carl Sorenson at SitesForContractors.com has been a great resource for us over the years, with very fair pricing, terms, and communication.

Ugly Fact-

If you insist on doing this on your own, you're going to waste a lot of time, and very likely hurt your brand. Pay the money, and do your research to make sure you're not getting ripped off. Ask about content generation, backlinks, and periodic search term updates.

- **Social Media**- FB, IG, Twitter are the types of platforms currently being used. In 10 years or less, this is likely to dramatically shift. The point is, maintain a public presence. You need to be posting content 2-3 times a week to stay at the top of the metrics from what we've been exposed to, but shoot for at least once a week consistently, with video content and a fair amount of text explanation as well.

Ugly Fact-

Social Media can and will be a complete waste of your time if you let it.

Like many other points in being an entrepreneur, be intentional about your time and energy with this, and pay attention to your local market. If your core market is a community that isn't on the Internet at all, your interactions online are going to look very different than an area where HOAs with open FB Groups and Moms are hiring remodeling contractors.

- **YouTube-** What if I told you you could have your own "TV channel" that focused viewers just on YOU. For free? Yep. That's essentially what YouTube gives you the ability to do. There's all kinds of video metrics and cute things to do with it. The key is vibrant content, arresting details, and good titles. We host a "Case Studies" playlist on our channel that allows us to share a focused data stream of videos that highlights our company's capabilities.

(This has been an invaluable part of communicating with potential clients! Sharing a successfully completed project that closely aligns with what their stated needs are gives us a great opportunity to A. Inform the client of our particular approach and B. Set the expectations for the services to be rendered.)

- **Be good at what you do.** There is an old proverb that says something along the lines of "if you see someone that's REALLY good at what they do, they will end up in the presence of kings." You're not going to start out at the very top of your game. We grow, mature, and learn as we go. That said, there should be a level of mastery/excellence of product/craft where it is a clear exchange of value, and not charity if people purchase your goods/services.

Storytime-

I learned my tradecraft from an ""old man.""

30 years in the industry, 20+ as a business owner, Rev. Dixon spent the better part of two years patiently teaching me the primary and secondary skills necessary to be an excellent drywall repair technician.

I certainly didn't start out of the gate looking like an expert; I had mud fall off my knife, grabbed the drywall knife handle like my life depended on it, was way too stiff and rigid, broke drywall knives by pressing too hard while trying to spread mud that was setting up....

The knife was not my friend.

I. Was. A. Mess.

My mentor's greatest gift?

His encouragement and belief in me.

"I think you've got the eye for this." That was really the only thing that kept me going for those first three months. Drywall finishing is an art; you can read about it, and even be shown it, but there is no substitute for actually doing the work to become proficient. I knew I was terrible at finishing, and it *killed* me. But after about six months, I was starting to get the hang of it. After two years, I was finishing drywall with the same proficiency of other folks at year three to five.

To this day, I am learning, growing, and doing my best to be faster, produce a better product, leave a cleaner jobsite, and put the client at ease.

Answer. The. Phone!

Yes, calls go to voicemail. However, do your best to answer the phone during regular business hours. If they call and don't leave a message, call them back! "This is Cathy from Cupcakes Supreme. We saw we had missed a call from this number, and were giving a courtesy call follow-up. How can we serve You?" Spoofing calls are rampant: however, you're better off doing your best to follow up with a client that didn't leave a voicemail than you are to ignore a call, making the assumption that it was spam.

Have an after-hours protocol.

Email and Text follow-up info.

It's quite simple to set it up, and it gives you a backup and search function on the next business day to make sure that you didn't miss anyone. "This is Sam's Detailing- We look forward to speaking with you about your project by the end of the next full business day. Please send over a couple photos of your vehicle, and we look forward to serving you!"

- **Communicate En Route-** This gives folks a "heads up," and is impressive to clients in today's age of service. So many times folks have gone with us because another company simply didn't follow through, show up, or give a call back. *Don't be that company.* A quick text message sent the evening before any appointment set over a week ago goes a long way towards making sure all parties are prepared for business. We like to send a reminder eta en route as well; this gives a last chance to catch a cancellation that you were unaware of.

- **Be Respectful**- Is there a guest bathroom to use during the course of your project? If not, where is the nearest gas station, porta-potty, convenience store? Is there any need to access any other parts of the house or property? Who is supposed to be on site while you are there? Are there any unusual hours to consider during the process, project, or event?

Storytime-

I had a helper. A good ol' country boy that worked with us a number of years ago. We were working in a hallway, had plastic up, and it was a pretty small working area. Instead of asking me if he could get by, "Buddy" excused himself, went outside, and relieved himself behind landscaping/shrubs in the side/backyard.

In city limits.

In a residential neighborhood...

And a pretty "well-to-do" one at that.

The client was a female, white collar, working professional.

So, yeah.

I was absolutely beside myself. At the end of the day, everything was done decently, nobody was offended or had any real issues, but MAN, just say "Excuse me" and we could have avoided that heart attack!

- **Cleanliness & Prep-** In the construction industry, a clean jobsite is a professional jobsite. Put up your tools, stage everything centrally each day. Use Zip Poles/ plastic sheeting to protect the rest of the home from debris/ dust migration. It adds a level of professionalism to the jobsite, gives separation of space from the contractor to homeowner, and a friendly rustle of introduction as someone enters the worksite.

In a store setting, have clean floors, no debris or trash on the floor, and clean windows.

Vehicle? Have it clean, smelling nice, in good running order!

Storytime-

On a commercial job years ago, I had a helper that was loaned out from the GC. The helper was tasked with cleaning the walls of old nails and screws, getting it ready for new sheetrock. I hear a "waterfall," walk across the building, and there is about a 4′ geyser about 18″ away from the main electrical panel of the commercial property! I had NOT planned on busting any water pipes, and as such, had failed to identify where the cutoff valve was to the building. I called up the site supervisor, and calmly asked where the water shut-off was...

"Why, did y'all break something?" he laughingly asked.

Yup.

We did.

We got the water shut off, nobody was electrocuted to death, and the fans and dehumidifiers were delivered and drying out the water we couldn't squeegee out the door in short order.

We were VERY fortunate that the building was essentially gutted, basically working with concrete and open walls at that point. It was a great lesson in preparation though- know where your water and electrical shut-offs are! Accidents happen, it's how you respond to them that defines your good name in business.

- **Use Good Faith Judgements-** Contracts go a LONG way, but at the end of the day, the integrity of the technician in a service business, or the salesperson at the register, is the ultimate test. Did you cut/pinch, chop a line? Were there undisclosed rot/mold issues? Did you truly provide the scope of services quoted? If it's a product, did you over-deliver, with intention? Did you make sure that breakage/defect parameters (in dealing with product delivery) are in favor of the client?

- **Trust & Verify Completion/ Delivery**- Have the client visually inspect, approve, and sign off on the work done/product provided. This insulates you from accusations, and keeps everyone on the same page.

To be honest, we are all human. Sometimes something little is just missed! A small bit of humility goes a *long* way; if a defect is identified, take care of it right then! Leave the jobsite cleaner than you found it. If you delivered the product versus providing a service, make sure that the yard/house/business is undamaged. Your packaging should be professional and clean. Many times, we like to use a handheld vacuum on our way out the door. It's a great way to impress the client, and it allows us to spot-clean any missed pieces of dust.

- **Take those Photos!** Take pictures, before, during, and after for your records. Consider submitting them into a cloud file for recordkeeping for your team. If there's a NDA in place, plan for that. And charge accordingly.

Storytime-

On a >$15k ceiling replacement over an indoor pool, we got a call AFTER we were all done. It seemed that there was a light missing, that had been there before.

Because it was a can light.

Annnnnndddd we covered it up.

By the grace of God, we DID have photos of the process of the project, and the layout of the lights was pretty consistent. Which was REALLY important, seeing as how the ceiling had already been painted. We cut a pilot hole, verified that the light WAS where we thought, and cut it out; No harm, no foul. That could have been a pretty involved follow-up call, but for a little bit of luck, and a whole lot of grace.

- **Ask for a Referral / Review with Intention.** Have your Google My Business up and running. Have your goods and services section filled out, with at least five reviews already online and posted. If you don't have five friends and family willing to vouch for your good or service, then it looks like you're doing some jobs for just about free to get those reviews going!

- **Thank You Gifts**- As appropriate, a thank you gift card or gift is a much appreciated way of expressing your appreciation for the folks using your services/ordering your product. It helps people to know you're not just a taker, but a person that truly values them.

- **Rinse and Repeat**- Continue to perfect your process, swag gifts, professional profile, etc.

Storytime-

The most formative thing in building a business (besides your faith and developing yourself) is the building of lasting relationships with good people. My good friend Rev. Ric Sears and I had a conversation some years ago about business, and after sharing with him a pretty aggressive approach to customer service that I held, he looked at me and basically said "that's not right." I disagreed, and backed it up with a bunch of big fancy words.

He was right, of course.

Taking care of people is what we are called to do as entrepreneurs.

Will you have situations and people that will try to take advantage of you?

Yes.

Being gentle with people builds a public view of value and approachability.

Don't be a doormat, but there is no need to be a porcupine roll of bathroom tissue either!

Becoming callous and rude to the needs of those closest to us is a recipe to be buried in a very nice coffin, with no one there to enjoy the party after.

Surround yourself with folks that are quality, that care for others, and that are willing to disagree with you.

CHAPTER 5

You Can Do It! (Even When You Fail)

To succeed, you must lead *yourself* with a "can-do" attitude. This is true for a family, a church, or a business. A can-do mindset helps you find answers, while a negative mindset only finds problems.

A can-do attitude has helped my wife and I through tough times. When we lived in a mobile home with very little furniture, Barbra used fancy cloth napkins to make our meals feel special. When we couldn't afford much meat, we figured out how to make a bag of meatballs last all week.

A “can-do” attitude is really about helping others; We will often do things for other people that we wouldn't (but should!) do for ourselves.

It feels terrible to be stuck, like you have no choices. When you feel that way, pick **one** part of your business and work on making it excellent. Then, keep looking for opportunities. Keep knocking on doors until one opens for you.

Storytime-

When my 1994 Jeep died in a client's driveway in an affluent neighborhood after closing a contract, I simply put it in neutral, pushed it around the corner, and flagged down a jump! When there was no drywall work, I found other jobs. I would work for 10 hours a day doing sod rip outs for $50.

A day.

Once, I (hilariously) tried to pick blueberries professionally...

One time that happened.

After three hours, I was still in the hole about $1.25 after my breakfast and gas. I called my wife pretty emotional, to be honest. "I'll try to do anything, but I can't make money at this." My hands were stained with little blue dots for DAYS afterwards.

I did whatever I could to make money for my family, and at least try to fight off the depression that comes with the disappointment of *wanting* to work and provide, and just not having many good options.

Ugly Fact-

There's a saying: If you look for problems, you will become an expert at finding problems. If you look for solutions, you will become an expert at finding solutions!

Sometimes, just saying the words, "We can do this," is all it takes to spark an idea, to find a way, and to take action.

Action-

What's a solution I can offer for a friend's company?

Would that same solution help my own company?

CHAPTER 6

Always Keep Your Promises

This seems simple, right?

But it's not.

It's easy to keep your word when everything is going along just fine. The real test is keeping your word when things are going wrong. I am sorry to say that I have failed at this before. At other times, I have succeeded.

Throughout this book, I want to tell you about failures, because that's how we learn.

And Remember the Lesson.

Early in one of our business ventures, we submitted to adjust the price on a customer's project (in the middle of a job) because it was taking longer than we thought it would. The customer was not happy, and they were right to NOT be happy!

See, I thought that the client would "see it my way."

I was dead wrong.

When you start looking for ways to change the value exchange to benefit yourself instead of serving the client, that's not honest.

That's not "swearing to your own hurt."

Another time, a very difficult customer was making professionally unreasonable demands- and we did not have a good exit clause in my contract. In the end, I chose to give them all of their money back. My company worked for a whole week for free. It was a painful lesson, but I "re-learned" how important a good contract is. I kept my promise to provide value, even though it cost me some money. The alternative would have been a very public and painful disclosure of a senior's altered mental status. So, drawing on past experience, we closed out the contract and left.

Our goal is to always give more value than what is expected.

My prices are not cheap, because life is not cheap, so I set a very high bar for myself and our business practices. You will come across situations as a business owner that will require a hard second look. For starters, consider before agreeing to the contract, is it profitable enough to take on "as is?" Or do some things need to be tweaked to make it work?

Storytime-

We received a phone call with follow-up texts for what would have been a perfect job for us- an indoor pool lanai ceiling replacement. The clients were given a rough heads up over the phone for what the anticipated replacement cost was likely to be based on past projects, and they were ok with what was presented.

During the project evaluation process, a disagreement arose as to whether or not a roof with a black color versus a white color would be hotter. At that moment, we decided that this client was NOT a good fit for us. We have worked for clients that wanted to be "in the driver's seat." They want to feel good about telling someone to do something. Not our favorite or first choice, but we bill them enough to make it worth our time.

When someone cannot (or will not?!) reasonably grasp the basic thermal properties of construction in a conversation, we are not going to go down that rabbit hole. It's not a good fit, and we're going to allow them the opportunity to pursue other industry options.

Sometimes, we will reconsider a project after reflection/prayer, and offer an extension of amended terms. VERY rarely does this work out- It *can*, but more likely than not, you're going to end up in a less-than-desirable position by the end of the project.

Ugly Fact-

Everyone wants to be a business owner until it's time to do business owner things.

If you CAN'T keep your word, don't give it!

CHAPTER 7

Making the Most of Your Time

Many successful people talk about how to manage time. My (admittedly stolen, thank you Pastor D.W. Autrey) take on this is simple: **we make time for the things that are important to us.**

Time is like a puff of smoke. You see it for a moment, but then it disappears. We can savor the aroma, the whisp, even value the beauty of it, but if you waste it, it's just gone. When we are smart with our time, we can build something wonderful. Good use of time builds on itself, creating more opportunities for us later.

Ugly Fact-

We don't need more time in the day. We need to get better at using the time we have.

Learning to invest, and not just manage, your time well expands your "blueprint" of success.

Think about it this way; if you manage your time correctly, it's like routing the water of a stream or a flood to keep damage from occurring. It reveals and adds beauty to the surroundings, and washes off the hard edges of things. If you INVEST with your time, it takes that management principle, and then turns it into power. Now, you are routing that water with purpose; you can run an electric turbine, provide water for a community, etc. When you can be trusted with time, you can be trusted with what we think of as "more important" things, like money and responsibility. Truly though, time is our most precious asset. It cannot be reproduced. It's only been recorded in history twice that it either "stood still" or moved backwards.

We must intentionally invest our time to become successful.

Storytime-

I have a routine that I follow almost every single day. My morning starts the same way, with time for coffee, prayer, and reading. I wear the same kind of clothes to work every day. A famous businessman once said he did this because he had to make so many other decisions during his day, and that by wearing the same outfit it was one less thing to think about.

Does this seem too strict? It might feel like it when you're just starting out and waiting for the phone to ring! But when you get busy, having a routine is the only way to get everything done efficiently.

The most important thing is to be **intentional**. That means you choose how to spend your time instead of just letting it slip away.

Start small. Wake up five minutes earlier for some quiet time. Soon, that will turn into ten minutes, then twenty, then an hour. If I can do it, you can do it.

Action-

Set your Alarm for Five Minutes Earlier than Today's!

CHAPTER 8

Your Business and Your Family

This part is really tough.

Being a business owner takes a lot of time and energy. It's easy to get home and have nothing left to give to your family. You have to be intentional and be available for them. For me, if I can give my wife and kids 45 minutes of my full, focused, undivided attention at least two to three times a week, it helps keep our bond strong. How much time can you give? *How much time does your family want?*

When you reach your goals, will anyone be there with you to celebrate?

People are not tools.

You can't just use them and throw them away.

People are precious.

You can help them shine by giving them your time and attention, or you can make them feel small by being harsh or ignoring them.

Whatever you decide your work-life "balance" is, choose it on purpose.

Ugly Fact-

It's often easier to do tasks at work than at home. At work, people thank you, and you get paid. At home, you're just "Mom" or "Dad." There is a never-ending list of chores: dishes, cooking, laundry, and bills. It's easy to spend all your happy energy at work, leaving only scraps for your family.

This is dangerous for relationships. We must make sure we are investing in our loved ones. Yes, there will be busy seasons and big projects. But don't mix up what is urgent with what is truly important. If you do, you might trade a real treasure, like your family, for a lot of trouble.

Storytime-

We took on a job with well over 700 sq ft of ceiling in an open concept ranch style home with 8' ceilings. The ceilings did have 1x4's running across the truss face, but were NOT leveled.

Instead of simply spending a couple hundred dollars on a laser, I thought I'd simply utilize string lines and get the ceiling flat.

Bad idea y'all.

I ended up backing out, shimming, and re-screwing that ceiling with about 7 lbs. of 3" Spax screws not once, not twice, but THREE times. I had NOT taken any time off, and as such was working to a point of sheer exhaustion. Adding insult to injury, I did not realize that the floor itself was uneven! My helper kindly put a board in place for me to install, and we ended up with a large section at the bottom crumpled up/ crushed when we went to install it.

I'm not super proud of the next part.

I kicked the rest of the sheetrock to death, told the helper to clean it up, and grab another sheet of drywall. To his credit, he did, and didn't say a word.

He also went home, lol.

Turns out when there's a 5/8" high spot in the floor, you end up having to carve that area out anyway. Take time to take a break. Breathe. The work will be there tomorrow; how we react in stressful situations can determine whether any staff will show up the next day!

CHAPTER 9

Where You Start Isn't Where You Have to Stay

We all start somewhere. But you don't have to stay there! The story of your life is written by the choices you make every day.

I started my drywall business out of the back of a 1995 Jeep Cherokee XJ. The air conditioning didn't work, and one day, the driver's side door fell right off! I screwed it back on with hinges I bought from a hardware store. That was my work truck.

How you look and what you have materially is both everything and nothing.

It is what is on the inside that really counts.

You can spend all your money trying to look successful, or you can make smart, careful choices that will help you build a business that lasts.

The fact is people do judge our competency based on how we look and present ourselves.

Having a uniform for your business is a great idea.

It tells people who you are and what you stand for.

It should be clean, functional, and have your company's name or logo on it.

Everyone on your team should wear one. It's a simple way to look professional and build your brand.

Storytime-

Early in my drywall business, I had an interesting project come to us. A residential structure had some fire-barrier / fire-wall that had failed, and we were being considered to provide the service needed. Awarded the contract, I found myself flat on my back in a Florida attic space at >/= 90°F, with nails protruding thru the roof sheathing approximately 3" from my face as I shimmied to and from the access available to install the fire tape. I ended up with blood on my scalp from the nails stabbing the back of my head.

I wanted to be able to be successful so bad, I counted the cost, and found it acceptable.

I traded temporary pain and blood for a lasting result. The financial success I found in taking on that and other challenging projects paved the way for me to be able to publish my first book. (It Hurts to Be Mad)

Side Quest

My first enclosed trailer for the drywall business was so small, a sheet of drywall wouldn't fit inside. We installed garage organization hardware on the outside of the trailer, and would wait until it wasn't raining to transport material. I simply used what I had, where I was, until better opportunities presented themselves.

You know someone that never looked down on me?

My vinyl lettering, business card, shirt guy.

Eric Burrus helped me on old vehicles, new vehicles, new trailers, trailers that should NOT have been being used...

He never made me feel small.

When something difficult is presented, look at it as an opportunity for success.

Does the contract require working overnight for a week?

Do it!

Does production need to be doubled to fill an order?

Take it on!

Make calculated decisions, but take the right type of risks.

What is that, the "right type of risk?"

It is an opportunity for financial progress and service to clients that stretches your established capacity to a point of near failure.

Make the hard decision, do the deal, make the sacrifice.

Action-

What is a "Right Risk" for your business you should take today?

CHAPTER 10

Business Look and Feel

Your brand is your business's personality.

It includes your logo, your name, and the feeling people on the outside of your organization get when they think about your company.

A good brand is like a flag that your team and your customers can rally around.

The best advice I can give you here is to **FAIL FASTER.**

What does that mean?

It means don't be afraid to try things and make mistakes! It took me about eight years and five different logos / variations to find the one we use today. Don't wait that long! Try an idea. If it doesn't work, learn from it and try something else. Get better, faster.

Your brand is so important.

Think about it: many brands are known for being high-quality, while others are valued for being cheap. Your brand is what your company is all about on the inside, showing on the outside. If you do excellent work, people will know you for that. If you cut corners, they'll know you for that, too.

Simple Marketing Ideas

- **Be Yourself:** Don't copy someone else. Be honest about who you are and what you do.
- **Get a Website:** A simple, professional website is a must. Make it easy for people to find your phone number or send you a message.
- **Use Social Media:** You don't have to be on every platform, but have a presence somewhere. Post pictures of your work at least a couple of times a week.
- **Set Up Your Google Business Profile:** This is so important! It's a free listing on Google. Fill it out completely and ask happy customers to leave you reviews. Good reviews help new customers trust you.
- **Network:** Get to know other business owners in your town. Building good relationships is key.

- Give Away Fun Stuff (Swag): Pens, t-shirts, or magnets with your logo on them are great reminders of your business.

- **Make a Video:** A professionally produced video shows people exactly what you do / sell. It will cost some money, but it can be a great investment.

When it comes to your logo, keep it simple. Don't use ten different colors and five different fonts. Make it clean, simple, and easy to remember.

Cupid the Curious Cat

I was working in a house where there was a very loved cat we will call "Cupid." He was very curious about the holes in the wall left over from the house being re-plumbed. Hired to patch those holes, I put the new drywall in, applied the adhesive mesh tape, and went home for the night.

The next morning the homeowner asked me if I had heard about what had happened last night:

The family couldn't find Cupid after we had left for the evening!

It was about 30 minutes or so after we left that they realized he was missing.

After 45 minutes of looking EVERYWHERE, they sat down on the couch, and they heard a tiny "mew."

It was coming from inside the wall, in the adjacent bedroom, behind the patch I had just installed!

The family quickly unscrewed the drywall patch to let him out, and the rest was PUBLIC history, as I had a seasoned leader delightedly tell the story to over 500 folks during a public event.

Some stories are too good to NOT be told!

People are going to talk about your company.

They will share how they felt, what their experience was, what happened, how it met or failed to meet their expectations, and whether they would use you again.

If you Mess Up, Fess Up.

If you receive negative feedback, respond back in the most gracious manner possible.

Many times, it is NOT the defect of craftsmanship or damaged good that sinks the relationship; No, it's how you respond to the "hiccup" that seals the deal.

CHAPTER 11

How to Talk About Your Business

When a potential customer calls, you need a quick and simple way to tell them who you are and how you can help. This is often called an "elevator pitch" because it should be short enough to say during an elevator ride.

Here's what I often say (more or less):

"*Hi! This is Daniel from DRR Drywall Repair. Thanks for calling! Tell me a little bit about your project.*"

Then, I explain what makes us different:

"*We are a State of Florida Licensed DBPR Drywall Contractor. We don't drink, smoke, curse, or do drugs. We specialize in seamless drywall repair and replacement in dynamic, occupied environments. If you HAVE to have these specific parameters for your project, we are typically a great fit. Our responsibility is to tell you the truth, and give you the data necessary to make an informed decision to make the right choice for your project.*

This little speech does two things. First, it tells the customer what we stand for. Second, it helps them decide if we are right for them. It sets the expectation that we provide high-quality work, and that our prices reflect that.

Your Unique Selling Point (USP)

Your elevator pitch should highlight your "Unique Selling Point," or USP. This is what makes you special. What do you do better than anyone else?

For my business, our USP is: **We are on time, our work quality is excellent, and we are consistent communicators.**

Figure out what makes you special, and make sure your customers know about it!

Action-

List three things that allow your business to stand out in the public's eye.

CHAPTER 12

Finding the Right Customers

You should use your elevator pitch to help you find the right customers. By being clear about who you are and what you do, you let people decide for themselves if you are a good match for their needs.

About 90% of the people who call my company don't end up hiring us. And that's okay! We either refer them to another contractor who is a better fit, or we teach them how to do the repair themselves. This is planned; we would go broke driving all over our coverage area to give estimates! Instead, we "qualify" our customers over the phone first.

Save Time with Remote Bids

Do you want to save THOUSANDS of dollars every year?

Stop driving out to every single call!

Years ago, I used to visit every potential job site. Now, technology helps us do a lot of that work from the office. We ask the customer to get involved by sending us pictures and measurements of the project.

We approach clients as if we are helping them solve a problem, not just trying to make a sale.

Ask for exactly what you need. For us, I ask for a couple pictures of the damaged area; to text the photos to us and then call us back by the end of the next business day if they have not heard from us.

Think about it: if a client isn't willing to take three minutes to send you a few photos, why should you spend an hour and a half driving to/from their house?

By having them do this small step, you find out who is serious about hiring a professional.

If the project is going to have lawyers involved or needing quotes for insurance purposes, we charge for that information! The quote is a necessary data input to accomplish the project, and because of that we engage in an exchange of value for our services.

Action-

What single question could you ask/add to your screening process to better serve your client's needs?

How do you approach a conversation with a potential client? Is it to make a sale? Solve a problem? Get to know them?

Is it working?

CHAPTER 13

What Are You Really Selling? Being a Specialist

The fastest way to lose a big, high-paying job is to say, "We do it ALL!"

Think about it-

When you need braces, your dentist sends you to a specialist called an orthodontist. If your car has a serious problem with the transmission, your mechanic might send you to the dealership, or a specialty shop. We trust specialists because they are experts at what they do.

So why **are** so many business owners afraid to specialize? Because they worry that if they don't do everything, they won't get any work!

Specializing lets you become an expert- you're able to provide more value and therefore charge higher prices. It took about 10 years for me to refine our marketing, sales, and craftsmanship in our drywall business. Then, I helped a partner start a new carpentry business, and we did the same thing in 62 days because we had learned this lesson.

Find a need in your community and become the very best at filling it.

My drywall company specializes in repairing and replacing drywall in homes and businesses that are occupied-

These are tricky jobs where you can't make a mess or be unprofessional. People are willing to pay for our expertise because *they know they are getting excellence.*

We don't paint.

We don't do trim.

We do one thing, and our goal is to do it so well that you can't even tell we were there. In short, when folks ask me what we do- "We repair and replace drywall in situations with a high opportunity cost."

That's what we *"DO."*

What is it that we sell?

Peace of Mind!

Price vs. Value

Always try to offer more value than your customer expects.

It doesn't have to be something big.

A friendly smile or an extra bit of cleanup can make a huge difference.

We recently did a sink of dishes before covering up the kitchen/masking off the work area.

Why?

Because we were paid enough to care about doing a quality job!

And, who expects a contractor to go the extra mile?!

It was an easy thing to do to give more value to the client.

Action-

What is something that you can do to add value to a client's order/ project that costs almost nothing?

Think about a customer service experience you had years ago that blew you away-

How can you imitate that in your business?

CHAPTER 14

Making Friends and Helping Each Other

There's a saying I love: "Great people do good business."

Ugly Fact-

Great people can be hard to find! If you want to be around excellent people, you have to be excellent yourself.

Be strategic about building relationships with other business owners.

You should check in with them regularly, maybe once a month. You don't have to be best friends with everyone, but you will need to build a network of people you can trust. One of these relationships led to a $9,000 job for my company!

Learn to say, "I'm sorry."

It can be hard for a leader to admit they made a mistake. But being able to apologize is a sign of strength, not weakness.

Referrals, which is when someone recommends your business to someone else, are the best kind of advertising.

A Referral is a Gift.

It means someone trusts you so much that they are willing to put their own reputation on the line...

Don't take that trust for granted.

If you do a great job, you build that trust.

If you mess up, you can break it very quickly.

If you're looking for a good way to meet other business owners, look for a local networking group. I have had a lot of success with a group called **BNI (Business Network International)**.

Dr. Ivan Misner started BNI over forty years ago with the goal of empowering and equipping entrepreneurs to grow their businesses through the power of accountability and referrals.

Dr. Misner, THANK YOU!

Building these relationships takes **TIME**.

You must become patient, consistent, and trustworthy.

CHAPTER 15

Taking Care of Your Money
Don't Spend Money That Isn't Yours

Many businesses will use a deposit from a "new job" to pay for an "old job."

Called "Floating," it is some kind of dangerous!

You are one bad day away from being unable to finish a job you've already been paid for.

It's borrowing without permission.

There's a word for that; it sounds a lot like "stealing."

Do whatever you have to do to get out of this habit.

Open a Business Bank Account

This is a huge step. You must keep your business money separate from your personal money. If you don't, you'll never really know if your business is making a profit, and is it your money, the business's money, Lord help us the client's money... No, You'll just have a big pile of money that you spend until it's gone, and then you've just got a mess.

Accountant / Accounting Software

Whatever you use, be consistent in it. After $100k of revenue a year, we found that a bookkeeper, and then a CPA, made sense to help us with our tax and accounting obligations.

Look into what revenue amount makes sense to pursue filing as an S Corporation in your LLC designation. We missed this critical point by one year- that cost us thousands of dollars!

NOTICE I SAID HELP

When you get audited as a small business, **your** signature, and **your** income is the one on the line.

Get an accountant you can trust. But you also need to begin to understand some of the terms used as well. A

P&L Statement. A Balance Sheet. Cash Flow. Liabilities and Assets.

Yes, these are big, scary concepts.

"I just want to work hard, and make money, and help my community and feed my family. I don't care about all of that."

Your ultimate success is tied to your understanding (or your successful subcontracting) of Financial Literacy.

If you're an established business owner, let me encourage you here- please at least brush over your Accounts Receivable, Major Purchases, Deposits, and Credit Card use monthly.

Quarterly, you need to be doing a "deep dive" with your financial team.

And every 6 months to a year, it is a "Best Practices" scenario to have an outside accountant look over things, to make sure nothing is falling through the cracks.

Storytime-

When team members have been a part of the company for a long time, they become family. That level of comfort can lead to financial disciplines being relaxed.

I personally know of a very smart white-collar professional that had a personal assistant that was in charge of running the business, paying for things, etc.

In the end, it was found out that they had taken money.

A LOT of money.

And it was over the course of years.

Independent eyes, periodic spot checks, and intentional financial accountability ensure that the company is healthy, and stays healthy.

Use a Credit Card Wisely: This might sound crazy, but we use a single business credit card for all our purchases. *Then, we pay the entire bill off at the end of every month.*

If there is a financial shortfall that means that the balance on the card cannot be reconciled with that period's earnings (whether due to a project pay/draw schedule or lack of business) we will work with business funds saved.

In a worst case scenario, we draw from a line of credit to temporarily float the shortfall and keep from being assessed high interest rates.

This helps us track our spending easily, and keeps our cash safe in the bank.

This only works if you are very disciplined.

If you are not good with credit, do not do this!

If the ONLY way you can pay your bills on time is to use an envelope system with cash, get to stuffing them full-

Pay Your Bills on Time!

Stay Calm in a Crisis

Life happens. Your work truck might break down. Your house might flood. When you are emotional and stressed, it's easy to make bad money decisions. In these moments, it's more important than ever to slow down *and get advice from people you trust.*

Ideally, you're looking for an entrepreneur that has at least five more years of experience than you do, in the same field of work, trade, or type of business.

Thoughts and dreams are wonderful, but make no mistake;

The man with the experience is never at the mercy of the man with the argument.

Experience is the Bedrock of Success-

Build on the Bedrock of Others!

Action-

Who do you know that owns or has owned the type of business you want to start or expand?

What day of the week is a good day to take them out to lunch or coffee, and pick their brain?

CHAPTER 16

Paperwork That Protects You- The Importance of Contracts

So important, we gave it its very own chapter, I have benefitted from having a written contract for many years. So many small business owners get into trouble because they have a bad contract, no contract, and/or don't even know that they need one!

If you are doing work for someone, you need a written, enforceable contract.

Period.

Mom? Contract.

Uncle? Contract.

Your Pastor? Contract.

It wouldn't hurt to have a contract in place when working on your own house with your spouse!

Why?

A contract clearly and expressly allows all parties to confirm, and then refer back to, the *intended* exchange of value and agreements made.

Why?

A contract protects everyone. It clearly states what work will be done, how much it will cost, and when it will be finished. It is a record of the facts. It's not about what someone remembers or what they think was said. Again, it is about the **facts**. At least, as they were recorded.

Storytime-

Learning how to negotiate, or agree on the terms of the contract, is a huge part of business-

It's where deals are made or broken.

One time, I lost a $2,000 job because I wasn't willing to give a small $100 - $200 discount.

It wasn't about the money; it was about my bad attitude.

I thought at the time that I was just "sticking to my guns." The job was going to be hot and challenging, and the services being provided were certainly in line with the bid presented.

I was trying to protect the exchange of value, but what I really should have done was *work with the client.*

I learned from that mistake; don't "nuke the deal" because you refuse to let the other person feel good about it.

Let the other guy feel good about it!!!

Invoices and Paperwork

An invoice is your bill to the customer.

You must send invoices to get paid.

Think of your business's cash as its lifeblood-

The invoice is the artery that lets the blood flow.

"The job isn't done until the paperwork is done."

This is so true.

Paperwork can feel overwhelming, but these are the capillaries that the cash will flow through!

Here's a great way to stand out to clients:

Keep all your important documents online in a place like Google Drive or Dropbox. You can create a single file with your business license, insurance information, and anything else a customer might need. When they ask for it, you can send it to them in seconds. This makes you look incredibly prepared AND professional!

Action-

Where do you keep all of your business documents?

Which online platform is most convenient for you to upload them?

What day this week are you going to take the time to get all those documents into a single online folder?

CHAPTER 17

Having a Team and Being a Good Place to Work

Hiring employees can be one of the most stressful parts of owning a business-

But having a team is what turns the J.O.B. you own into a real business!

Storytime-

When I was a teenager, I worked at a local deli.

The owners treated me like family-They were kind, fair, and supportive. When I left that job, they threw me a party and gave me a watch. I didn't do anything noteworthy, except show up, work hard, and be honest.

I was late about 4-6 times in 2.5 years.

The money bag for deliveries that I was in charge of, plus tips, was only ever short twice- (I must have had a large bill that stuck when giving change.)

They trusted me.

The inclusion of being a part of a team, of being loved and valued...

I'm telling the story a ¼ century later.

How You Treat People Matters.

I have tried to be that same kind of boss in my own companies.

Being "kind" hasn't always worked out, as far as it benefitting the bottom dollar.

I have learned that it's better to pay people based on their performance, not just an hourly salary, or with an idea of how hard you think (or they say) they will work.

My advice and experience?

Pay your employees well and always, **always** pay them on time.

It is your job as the owner to make sure there is money in the bank to pay your team.

Not their responsibility-

YOURS.

Company Culture

"Culture" is the feeling of what it's like to work and interact inside the "walls" of your company.

If you have a workplace full of gossip and negativity, good people will not stay for long.

Storytime-

In construction, there's a lot of joking around. That's okay, as long as everyone *ultimately*feels supported and respected. At the end of a long, hard day of physical labor, it's the friendships with your coworkers that make the job enjoyable and build a strong team. Cat-Pee Feet, Tridgid, Oh the Gelatony of it All, Foggin' Off, Super Necessary... Every job has a story behind it.

At our drywall company, we came up with an acronym for being a Boss- Being Other's Strong Support.

That's what we are called to do, to strengthen, uphold, impart. Not to advantage ourselves of others.

Side Quest

Tim is my friend.

Well, a little more than that-

See, Tim is my Brother in Christ.

He's also one of those happy-go-lucky, absolutely hysterical guys with a GREAT personality and sense of humor.

One day, he tagged along with me on a back porch ceiling replacement as a favor.

We were working on installing a new board, and it just would NOT line / go into the space correctly.

I worked with it, and worked with it...

Until I had enough.

I chunked it away from me to the ground Captain America-style over my head, looked at Tim and said "WE'LL GET ANOTHER BOARD."

Tim?

He thought that was absolutely hysterical.

Me?

Not so much.

But when Tim starts laughing, you can't HELP but join in!

Sometimes you are GOING to be frustrated- a friend that's there for you in the trenches can make the world of difference.

Being a good place to work starts with being a good person to work with.

If you're on edge, sleep deprived, have a bunch of stuff happening personally with relationships, legal problems on your mind, issues with substance abuse-

You're going to have a tough time keeping clients happy, much less building a team of people that want to be around you.

Find ways to laugh at yourself.

Embrace your flaws.

Be open with your own shortcomings.

Put others in a position to succeed, and give them the spotlight.

Action-

What is something I can do on my jobsite, for my client, or include with my product that would make it a nicer environment for everyone?

Conclusion

So, here we are!

You've had a front row seat to some of our successes, and a fair amount of our failures.

My goal is for you to take the stories and lessons in these pages, and build the very best business that you can.

That starts with your **Action.**

Build a brand of excellence.

Make a name for yourself and your family that you can be proud of.

Be honest, fair, and consistent.

Build a New Business from the Small Space you are in.

GROW.

Made in the USA
Monee, IL
04 November 2026

67377665R00059